14 Days to a We..

Chandler Jeffries

rev6.22.13

www.BellaMediaPublishing.com

Visit Us:

Facebook: http://facebook.com/bellamediapublishing

Disclaimer

This book is intended for educational purposes only and does not replace a consultation with a certified animal trainer, veterinarian or other qualified animal professional.

Insider Bonus

In just 14 days you will have a better behaved and well trained dog but I know you won't want to stop there. After your initial training, be sure to download your complimentary bonus chapter at http://wellbehavedin14days.com.

Chapter 1

Introduction

Why Train Your Dog?

As a dog owner, we all have dreams of the perfect dog. Your family pet and best friend that listens to your every command, cheers you up when you're feeling down and is there for every important family event.

Your perfect dog that greets you happily each day when you arrive home from work, tail wagging and that silly grin on her face. It's what so many dog owners dream of when they pick up that new puppy from the breeder or from the shelter. Soon they find out that having a dog, better yet, the perfect dog, takes a little bit of work.

If that's your dream, you're in luck because it's achievable. In fact, it's achievable in the next 14 days.

The reason you must train your dog isn't just to make your life easier - it's to make their life easier. Dogs love being trained. They thrive on the mental stimulation, the excitement and the attention. Even more importantly though, a well-trained dog keeps you, your family, your guests and your new four-legged friend, safe.

When you train your dog the right way, they will be well-behaved and a joy to be around. Your dog will be easy to get along with and will come to know what to expect when others are around and what you expect of them.

The excitement of being able to give your dog or puppy a command and have them complete the task is a great feeling. It will give you a great sense of accomplishment and energize you to want to rush and teach your friend new tricks.

While training is simple, it isn't always easy. The steps I've laid out in this book build upon each previous step to guarantee your dog will pick up each new command and help provide a happy safe home for everyone in your family.

Just imagine, in the next 14 days, you will be able to give a hand signal and have your dog sit, lie down, come when called or even go to their mat or bed without hassle or headache. In fact, in the next 2 days you will already be showing off just how smart your new dog or puppy is to everyone that will watch.

Before we begin, you need to understand a little of the basics of training and why what I'm about to show you works so well.

Chapter 2

Understanding Training Methods

There are different training methods and styles. Each method has its place and time when it can be used appropriately.

The basics of positive reinforcement

Positive reinforcement training has been developed over the years and it's based on a reward system. The training is built upon the premise that your dog will perform commands and learn when they realize they will receive a reward. Think of Pavlov's dog. When the dog heard the bell, he knew he would be fed. As a result, every time the dog heard the bell he began to salivate in anticipation of food.

Positive reinforcement training works the same way. You will issue commands to your dog and eventually teach them the action. When they perform it correctly, they are rewarded. The positive reinforcement encourages them to complete the command.

What is negative reinforcement?

Negative reinforcement isn't quite the opposite of positive reinforcement training. In positive reinforcement training, the dog is completing a command because they know a reward is coming.

Negative reinforcement training puts the emphasis on the dog being scolded to not perform certain tasks. For instance, when a dog pulls on a leash, some trainers will "pop" the leash which shocks or scares the dog. Over time, they learn not to pull and will ease up. Whereas with positive reinforcement, when a dog is not pulling on the leash you reward them for being a good dog and continue walking. When they pull on the leash, you stop and when you walk successfully, you reward.

In this book we are going to focus on positive reinforcement.

Motivating your dog

The key to effectively training your dog is to understand what motivates them. This is not likely going to be a single thing or action. It will be many. Most dogs are motivated by treats as their reward. However rewards can also be a game of fetch, a belly rub, a "Good Girl" pat on the head, a quick game of tug or a favorite toy.

Watch what it is your dog enjoys and make note of it. This is going to come in handy as you begin training.

Just remember, that once you determine your dogs' motivation, they don't get that on a daily basis for doing nothing. They MUST EARN it. I want to put emphasis on the words must earn. Going forward, this motivation, whether it's treats or playtime, is an earned reward where your dog must perform to get rewarded. Otherwise, they will come to expect the reward for doing nothing.

If treats are your dogs' motivation you should keep in mind that you won't always need to treat. Treats are used heavily in the beginning of training. As your training progresses, you can begin substituting treats for praise.

A Puppy's Attention and Old Dogs/New Tricks

The age of your puppy is an important factor to keep in mind when training. If your puppy is young you will see that they really can accomplish everything in this book in just 14 days. However, just like young children, young puppies also have a very short attention span. The younger they are, the shorter your training sessions need to be.

However, as you continue to work with your puppy, you will begin to see remarkable improvements in attention times and their ability to perform commands longer. (Like holding a "Stay" command for 3 or more minutes.)

Slightly older dogs, between 8 months and 2 years old, are still considered puppies, but are more like teenage dogs. They are enthusiastic and energetic, but also lose focus very quickly as well. That's why it's so important to take your time and focus on the basics in this book first.

Older dogs can very easily pick up new tricks and learn the basics if they have never been trained before. They can also relearn tricks, hand signals and commands regardless of what they have been taught before. Don't worry about that old saying, "You can't teach an old dog new tricks", it couldn't be further from the truth.

Being Patient and Understanding your dog

Just like you want your dog to be patient and listen to your every command and learn everything immediately, you must be patient as well.

By the end of your Day 1 training session, you may feel that your dog already has a solid understanding of what the clicker sound means. Even a day later, when your dog is now quickly sitting and looking for a reward, you may have the inclination to move ahead to the next command. Don't.

One of the biggest mistakes people make when training their dog is to believe their dog understands the new command and stops the training too soon. As much as you want to rush, you must be patient. That means taking your training slowly, being patient with your dog and always understanding when they are losing interest or focus.

Don't rush your training and always follow the steps I'm about to lay out for you. Even if you feel your dog has mastered the command, it's important to continue the training each and every day.

Each command will build upon the previous and it is very important that she knows and can execute the command each and every time. Repetition will create the perfection and well-behaved dog you are trying to develop.

The Types of Training

In a few of the commands and exercises I'm going to explain different training styles. Some may work better for your dog because every dog is different. In our 14 day training we will mostly use luring, shaping and capturing methods. I've explained each and how they may work better for your dog.

Luring is exactly the way it sounds. We will be luring your dog to perform a specific command or behavior through the use of a treat. This works well for commands such as sit, down and stand. Luring commands are great for starting out, but once you get the dog to perform the command you will want to stop luring and rely on the voice commands and hand signals.

Shaping is a method that allows your dog to experiment and learn what it is you are asking of it. For instance, you may have your dog in a sit position and grab her paw. You will then click and treat her. You'd then put her paw down and repeat the process. She will eventually understand that she will receive a treat when she puts her paw in your hand, thus teaching her to "Shake".

Capturing is a method of waiting for your dog to perform a specific action and Clicking, or marking, the action and then treating. For example, some trainers will teach a "sit" command by simply waiting for the puppy to sit on their own. When the puppy sits, the action is "marked" with a click the moment her hind quarters touch the ground and she then receives a treat. The command "Sit" is added. You then move and allow the dog to follow. When she sits on her own again you repeat the process. She will begin to understand that she gets treated for sitting and will associate the command you give her with the action and the treat.

Modeling is the last of the training types and is the least helpful. This method essentially requires you to force or push the dog into a specific command or position. Ultimately, this sort of behavior will usually have your dog working against you instead of with you. It's for that reason we will be skipping that type of training.

Clicker Training

Throughout this training, we will be using the clicker training method. This is also called Marker Training. Marker training is where we will be marking an action when it is performed and then rewarding. Keep in mind that we are marking the behavior when it happens and immediately treating or rewarding the dog. This happens within 1 second or less of the action. Marker training uses a simple "Mark" or an "OK" or "Yes" type praise. Using the clicker we are simply replacing a verbal mark with the click.

Using a clicker is one of the most reliable and easiest methods for training because it's consistent. Often people will interchange their marking words, losing the consistency. Consistency, patience and timing are critical for training.

To effectively use clicker training we will want to perfect the timing of the click. A moment too soon and your dog will not grasp what command or action you are looking for. A moment too late and your dog will not hold or complete the command because they will be rushing through the action to get a reward. That's why timing is so important.

For example, with the sit command, we want to click the moment your dog's hind quarters touch the floor. After the click, you treat and release. The release portion is also very important. You must mark the end of the command as well. I always use "OK" as my release word. It's also important throughout the training to stick with the same release word. This will be important through sit, stay, down and the other commands.

To review, our clicker training steps will look something like this initially:

Lure ➡ Command Performed + Verbal Command + Hand Signal ➡ CLICK ➡ Treat ➡ Release

Now that you have the basics, let's get started.

Don't forget your bonus chapter that contains more tips and tricks.

Download it for free today at *http://wellbehavedin14days.com*

Chapter 3

Getting Started

Everything You Will Need

Now that you have the basic understanding of what we will be doing it's time to get your supplies. You will really only need a few basic training items and should always have these items close by.

The Clicker
There are many different types of clickers available. Some are fancy with bracelets to keep your clicker handy when training, and others are very basic plastic clickers. The choice is yours, but I've always used the inexpensive clickers found at pet stores near the checkout for a few dollars. Those work just as well as the expensive clickers, and if they are lost or broken they are easy to replace.

Small, Soft Treats
Many people try to train with old fashioned milk bone dog biscuits. This is not the best option. You should use small, soft treats that your dog can chew and swallow quickly, and that won't fill them up. These treats are really only used to give your dog a taste of the reward. I recommend using small dog training treats and breaking them in half. These treats are the size of M&M's and are perfect for any size dog.

The Collar

The collar you choose should be flat with a buckle or clasp. You should not use choke or prong collars during training. Always be sure that you have an identification tag attached to your dogs' collar with their name and your contact details. You will use the collar during leash training and as a light guide for helping your dog into position.

Leash and Lead/Rope
You will need a 6 foot nylon or rope leash. Do not use retractable leashes because those types of leashes always keep tension on your dogs' collar. When leash training, you will want your dog to be accustomed to the feel of a loose leash.

You will also want a 25-40 foot rope to use during the "Stay" and "Come" training sessions.

Tennis Ball or Other "Distraction"
Finally, you will need a small distraction for your dog. This distraction will be used when you begin testing your dogs' focus and duration for stay, come and other commands.

Final Tips for Training

Keep your training simple and fun. If it's not fun for you or your dog you will both lose interest and training will be difficult to finish.

Use short bursts of training. Keep your training times to 20 minutes or under when first starting out. You should be able to gauge your dogs' interest and focus based on her responsiveness and whether she is interested or not.

Be realistic and set your own expectations. Remember that this is all brand new to your dog (and maybe you), so set realistic expectations. Don't expect her to master everything in the first 5 minutes of training.

She's no genius, or is she? You'll quickly realize that your dog is quite smart and you'll begin to see her connecting the click with the reward and your command. Be patient.

Don't rush. Throughout this book you've heard it repeated several times - you must be patient and not rush through training. Take your time with your training and dog and you will see results.

Mix in real situations. Even when you're not in "training" you should be emphasizing what you've taught your dog. Use the sit command before you put down her food bowl or make her sit when putting on her leash. The more often your reiterate the commands she's learning in real life situations the quicker she will become the well-behaved dog you've been dreaming about.

No food before training. Since you will be training with treats as rewards you must ensure that your dog is interested in the reward. Always train before you feed her so she will stay interested in the training.

Chapter 4

Consistency and Patterns

Being consistent is very important, especially when you are training a family pet and there will be multiple family members involved. You should always use the same tone in your voice, say the command the same way and use the same words and hand signals throughout training.

Nothing can be more confusing for your dog than to receive three different commands and expect to know they all mean the same thing.

Remember, don't change your tone, how you talk or your hand signals. They must be consistent from person to person.

Never repeat yourself or the command. When giving your dog a command you must say the command, give the hand signal and wait. Saying "Bella, Sit, Sit, Sit!" is not the same as "Bella Sit". Repeating the command over and over only shows the dog that she's in control and can listen when she wants to. If you find that after 10-15 seconds you are not getting a response you must get your dog's attention and begin the command again. I discuss getting the focus on Day 1 of your training.

Always click and treat. Timing is everything. Never, click and not reward, especially in the beginning of your training sessions. When to click and when to treat is very important. Make sure that each person involved in your training understands the timing.

Never use the clicker as a recall device. What I mean by that is you should never use the clicker as a way to call your dog from the yard or from across the house. The clicker is used to mark a specific learned behavior. It's true that your dog will learn that hearing the click will often be followed by a treat and they will come running, but that's now how we want to teach that specific response.

Mix up rewards by using treats and praise. Initially you will only be using treats to reward your dog. As training progresses you will want to mix in a "Good girl!", a head pat or some extra love in place of treats in order to condition your dog that she will not always receive a treat.

It's time! On to day 1 training.

Chapter 5

Day 1 – The Basics, Look at Me!

It's day 1 and I know you're excited to get started. You've likely rushed and skimmed through the first few chapters just to get here and get started. If that's what you've done, I encourage you to go back and read the first few chapters in order to ensure you get the full picture of what we're going to be doing.

It's important on day 1 to be patient and take your time. Day 1 will have two sessions, morning and night. These will be dedicated sessions. In between those times, you will be practicing and reiterating in an ad-hoc/real life training environment.

What you need: Clicker, treats and patience!

Before we jump into teaching the sit command we need to teach your dog about the clicker and the rewards. This is the fun part and when you really get to see how your dog is going to react during training.

Charging the Clicker

To begin, we are going to charge the clicker or give your dog the understanding that the clicking sound is a good thing.

Set yourself up for success by removing all toys, bones and other distractions. Be sure your dog hasn't eaten and let's begin.

Have a treat in your hand and simply click the clicker and immediately give her the treat. Upon treating, give her a "good girl" and then ignore her.

The first click and treat will come as s surprise and she's going to be looking for more. Don't give her any when she's looking for a treat, just wait. When she's not paying attention, click again, treat and say "good girl".

Repeat the process 5-7 times.

You should begin to see her connecting the click with a treat. Upon a click, she's going to give you her attention. That's progress! We've now gotten her to understand that the click signals a reward is coming. Now we want her to focus on you.

Look at Me

Eye contact is a huge part of communication between people and animals. It's very important between you and your dog. When giving your dog commands, we want to know that we have her attention and focus, and we will accomplish that by making eye contact.

As we move forward with the close up commands like sit, down, stay, shake etc., we will want eye contact. Here's how we accomplish this.

Take a treat in your hand and hold the clicker in your other hand. Simply click and treat to engage her. Now that you have her attention we want her focus.

Using another treat, wave it slowly in front of her nose so that she gets a good sniff and knows there's a treat in your hand. Her nose and eyes are going to follow your hand wherever you move it.

Slowly move your treat hand from her nose, up to your face and point at your nose. When your hand arrives at your face and her eyes are looking at yours, say "Watch me" or "Look at me", then click and treat. Be sure you are standing straight and tall. Never bend or crouch to give your commands.

Now repeat the "Look at me" command. Each time use the treat to get her attention and to look into your eyes. Click and treat with the verbal command.

Over time, you will simply be able to say, "Bella, look at me", and point at your nose. Her eyes should meet yours and you will then be ready to give her your command.

Practice the "Look at me" and charging commands on day 1. Day 2 brings the excitement of your first command and results.

Chapter 6

Day 2 - The Most Important Command, Sit

There are 2 methods for teaching "Sit" and both are really easy to follow and teach. One is by luring, the other by capturing. I'll cover both, but in my opinion, luring is the best and easiest and will likely give you the best results.

What you need: Clicker, treats and patience!

Before you begin, I do want to point out one thing you should never do. You should never try and force your dog into a sit position by pushing their butt to the floor. Trying to do this will actually force your dog against your hand and try to remain standing. As tempting as it may be, don't do this.

Using Luring – Take a small treat in your right hand and have the clicker in your left. Move the treat toward your dogs' nose and then begin slowly raising it up over her head. Her butt will instinctively lower into a sit position as she raises her head to follow the treat. The moment her butt hits the floor, click and give her a treat. At this time, we aren't giving any voice or hand signals.

Once she has taken the treat, and hopefully still sitting, say "OK" and move away. She will get up and follow you.

Repeat the process with another treat. Again, timing is everything. Click and treat the moment her butt hits the floor. Have her hold the sit position and then say "OK" again and move away so she gets up.

If she backs up and remains standing, don't worry, simply reset and start again. If she continually backs up and never goes into a sit command, try positioning her so when she backs up, she will run into a wall with her butt. She will then sit.

After 2-3 successful attempts, we will now incorporate the verbal command and the hand signal.

The hand signal is your hand opened flat, palm facing the sky. The easiest way to issue the command is to hold the treat between 2 fingers while keeping your hand open. Allow the dog to smell the treat and now raise your hand up slightly as before as she begins to sit.

The moment her butt hits the floor say "Sit". Click and treat.

Repeat 10-12 times. Always be sure to always be consistent.

In the second training session later in the day we will immediately begin with the hand signal and verbal command at the same time. Session two will last 10-12 treats and we will mix up treats with praise.

Remember that even when you aren't in a training session to reiterate the commands. For example, before you feed your dog, make her sit.

Capture the Sit

More patience is required to capture the sit command. With capturing, we are waiting for the dog to sit on her own. This is usually easier with puppies.

You must patiently wait for the dog to sit. The moment her butt hits the floor you click and treat. Once she does this a few times she will understand that when she sits, you click and treat. Now add the hand signal and voice command at the same time.

After 8-10 treats she will begin to connect the hand, voice and action together. Click and treat.

In the second session you can immediately begin with the voice and hand signal.

Always practice with praise. Even outside of your normal structured training sessions always encourage your dog to sit. When she does, give her plenty of praise and an occasional treat. Putting the sit in real world experiences demonstrates your expectations for her and allows her to get praise and love for you outside of the normal training.

Chapter 7

Day 3 – It's Time to Lie Down

We begin on day 3 picking up with the "Sit" command. We will want to only spend 3-5 treats reiterating the sit command and then move directly into the down training session.

What you need: Clicker, treats and patience!

The down command begins with the sit. To prepare, have a treat in your right hand and put her into a sit. Put your hand in front of her nose and slowly lower the treat to the ground.

As she gets lower to the ground her body will naturally fall into a lying position. You've just accomplished the down position. Be sure to click and treat the moment she is in the down position and give her a treat.

Just as with the sit, we want to end the command by releasing her with an "OK".

Don't confuse "Down" with "Off". Many people will yell "Down" when their dog jumps on people or counter surfs. It's important to be consistent. "Down" should be the lie down command and "Off" is getting off of people, furniture or counters.

Now we want to repeat the process. Move away and get her back into a sit position. Here we are reinforcing the sit, and then leading into the down. Repeat the process 2-3 times. She should be catching on.

Now we want to add the hand signal and voice command.

The down hand signal is an index finger pointed downward. The easiest way to show this is to hold the treat between your index finger and thumb in a downward pointing position. Say "Down" while moving the treat hand downward toward the floor. Click, treat and release.

As time goes by you, will not need to move the treat to the floor. Simply pointing down and issuing the command is enough. Always click and treat when she has completed the action. Don't forget to release.

Practice this in at least 2 more sessions during the day. At each session try not move the treat to the floor and allow her to immediately go down without the incentive of the treat.

Eventually we will be able to issue the down command from her standing without even going into a sit position.

Remember to practice your commands outside of a normal training session. You may want to substitute verbal command for just hand signals and vice versa to reinforce the training.

Chapter 8

Day 4 – Will You Come Here, Please?

Here we are on day 4 already and it's time to add some action and playfulness to your training. Today we are going to reiterate the first two commands, "Sit" and "Down" throughout our training, but we are also going to add in the "Come" command.

This is one of the single most important commands a dog and pet owner can master. The "Come" command can save your dogs' life and keep them out of harm's way. It's also one of the single most prominent and proud moments when you can call your dog from anywhere and they will come on command.

It's very important that you only perform this command in safe area. Do not try and train near a busy street or areas when your dog can potentially run away. Always be safe.

What you need: Clicker, treats, short lead or leash.

The "Come" command can be done in two different manners, alone or with a partner. I prefer the partner approach because it adds an element of excitement and playfulness for your dog.

We'll start with training her alone. For this exercise we are going to need a 6 foot leash or rope. We do not want a retractable leash, only a long nylon or cotton lead or rope.

You'll need some treats and your clicker ready and have the leash attached to her.

Now start by putting her in a sit command. Now take 1-2 steps back and immediately say "Come Bella" Obviously, substitute your dog's name here. The moment she starts moving toward you get excited, but don't' click or treat yet. When she arrives at your feet, click and treat. Put her in a "Sit", click and treat.

Repeat this 2-3 more times. By the fourth or fifth time, you should begin taken larger steps and be further from her. This will allow for more space. Always click and treat when she arrives. If she pauses or hesitates give a little tug on her leash and get excited again while calling her with "Come, Bella". When she arrives, click and treat.

Short distance training for the "Come" command can be done indoors. When we get to calling from a distance we will want to move an outdoor, enclosed area.

Two People

Teaching her the "Come" command with two people is a bit easier. One person is the holder and the other is the caller.

The caller will have the clicker and the treat. The holder will be hanging on to her leash, keeping her in place.

We start with both the holder and caller in the same location and putting your dog in the sit position. The caller will then move away around 10-20 feet while the holder keeps her in position. I've found that if the caller runs away, it builds up excitement for the dog to want and chase after her. Until you are ready, the holder should not release or let go of the dog.

When the caller has reached their distance they will turn and say "Come Bella" while slapping their knees and getting excited. Now it's time for the holder to release the dog and your dog should immediate run to you. As soon as she arrives at your feet grab her leash, click and treat, then put her in a sit position.

Always grab her leash first, then click and treat. This insures she won't get free again.

Now repeat. Eventually you won't need to build the excitement by running away; simply saying "Come Bella" will be enough. Always grab her leash when she arrives and be sure to click and treat.

Repeat this process.

If you find that she stops or gets distracted midway on her way toward you, encourage her with more knee slapping and calling. You may want to shorten the distance as well.

The hand signal for the "Come" command is your arm raised outward and bent at a 90 degree angle as if you are motioning her to come toward you. Many people also use slapping on their knees. Both work, and unless you are in a competition, I tend to go with what is more comfortable. Always teach a hand signal in the event you are calling your dog from a distance and she may not be able to hear you.

Never, ever call your dog and then scold her. She will then connect coming to you with being scolded and may never come when called.

Continue to practice the "Come" command inside and from shorter distances.

A great exercise for daily use is when it's time to go out. Call her using the "Come" command, put her in a sit position and then attach her leash to go out. Doing this each time you take her out will set the expectation of what you want from her each time she goes out.

Chapter 9

Day 5 – Getting Here Quickly

Day 5 has arrived and you should already be seeing some great results from your dog. By now, your dog should be able to sit and lie down on command without any type of treat luring or encouragement.

You should also be regularly putting your dog in a sit command before they go out and before you feed them. You may also wish to get them in the habit of sitting before any guest pets them or greets them. This will help calm your dog when greeting people.

Today we are going to continue working on the come command, but in a slightly different way. Today, you will be calling your dog without them seeing you. It's a bit of a game for them, but you want to also get them in the habit of hearing your voice, your tone and understanding the command.

What you need: Clicker, treats.

I recommend conducting this training inside your home if space permits. If you are working alone it will be a little more difficult, but can still be fun.

Working Alone

First, you will want her to know it's training time. Begin by putting her in a sit command, click and treat.

Now slip away unnoticed to a different room, but not too far. Call her with the come command and continue to encourage along the way. She may not be able to see you, but she will hear your voice.

Once she arrives, click and treat. Give her lots of praise. Now repeat the training again by slipping away.

Two People

Two person training is a bit easier. Again, one person will be the holder and the other person will be the caller. Be sure that your dog knows it is training time by putting her in a sit command, clicking and treating.

The caller should now move to another room while the holder is keeping the dog in place. The caller should now give the command, "Come Bella". Continue to encourage her as she gets closer. It's a bit like hide and seek.

Continue to increase the distance throughout the house using only the voice command. Always click and treat when she arrives.

Remember to practice and bundle all of your commands in real life situations.

The "Come" command is by far the most important and the one that can really save your dogs' life. Also practice it and use whenever you call your dog.

Remember, never call your dog to you using the come command and then reprimand her. This will only cause her to not come when called and could cause bigger behavior problems.

Tomorrow we are going to focus on calling her from a distance in an open area outside.

Chapter 10

Day 6 – From Across the Park

Today is a big day. It's day 6 and we are moving outside to begin calling your dog from a distance. Now the distance is going to be relative to your dogs' age and size. For a puppy or a smaller dog, fifty to one hundred feet is a lot. For an older or adolescent dog, fifty to one hundred feet is perfect.

However, before you move on to calling your dog from a distance you want to be comfortable that she has successfully mastered coming when called on day 5 and understanding the come command in general.

What you need: Clicker, treats, leash and a long rope, enclosed area.

This will be the most nerve wracking and stressful of your training days. Today you will turn her lose and have her come to you when called.

Before you begin, I want you to remember that dogs and puppies can sense your frustration, your fear and your stresses. It's those senses that make dogs such great companions. It's also those senses that make it difficult for some people to be able to successfully train their dogs.

If you're stressed or have anxiety about whether your dog will come to you, let it go. We're going to put safeguards in place that will help with your training and help boost your confidence. Today is that day.

To begin, we want to attach a rope that's approximately fifty feet long to your dogs' collar. You'll want this just in case your dog stops or strays. If you're in an enclosed, safe area you can forego the rope, but I like it to coax her along if needed.

Teaching the come from a distance requires two people. One person will be keeping her in place while the other person gets into position and is ready to call her.

As you begin, be sure as the caller moves away and that they bring the end of the rope with them. Again, the rope only serves 2 purposes, to retrieve your dog if they take off from the training area or to help coax them along with a little tug.

Let's start with a little excitement. Have the one person hold the dog while the other person, the caller, runs approximately fifty to one hundred feet in one direction holding the end of the long rope.

Turn and say "Come Bella", obviously substituting your dog's name for Bella. The holder should immediately release the dog and she should begin to take off toward you. As she's running toward you, encourage her with lots of praise, knee slapping and excitement.

If for some reason she stops, you can give her a small tug on the rope, or continue to encourage her with lots of praise and excitement.

When she arrives, be sure to secure her by grabbing the rope or lead, clicking, treating and praising.

Now repeat.

Teaching the coming from a distance is a great way to exercise your dog and get her excited about coming when called. You should keep in mind that this particular exercise is also one that she may become bored with quickly. You'll want to pace yourself and maybe shorten your training sessions to 5-10 minutes at most.

Always be sure to mix in your hand signals and voice commands with each training session.

Once you are fully confident your dog will obey your commands, you can remove the long rope lead. Again, remember that having confidence in your training goes a long way.

Most dog owners recognize that they will rarely need to call their dog from a distance, but it's always when you least expect it that you need it the most. Having trained her to come when called, especially from a distance will be the life saver for you.

Chapter 11

Day 7 – Don't Go Anywhere, with Ease

Congratulations on completing the first week of training. By now you and your dog should have mastered the first three major commands.

It's now time to add one of the most helpful commands to your arsenal, the "Stay" command.

Out of all of the commands, stay requires the most patience, but is one of the most rewarding and useful for your dog. Today, you're going to accomplish the stay command with ease.

What you need: Clicker, treats, leash and patience.

It will be most helpful to read the entire process of teaching your dog to stay before actually trying to teach her. This is because different dogs have different attention spans and may require a bit more training and tries before you increase your distance.

To start, you will put your dog in a sit position in the location of your choice. Try to choose a location with very few distractions as the first few sessions will require her complete concentration.

Once she's in a sit and you are facing each other, you will give her the stay command while showing her the stay hand signal, your hand facing her, palm downward as if you are tell her to "stop", but keeping your hand at a 45 degree angel. Once you issue the command, take one big step backwards, pause for a second, step forward, click and treat. Give her praise, and then release her with an "OK" or your release word.

You've just completed your first stay command.

If she happened to get up and follow you as you step backward, gently return her to the exact location you start from, issue a sit command quickly followed by a stay command, and repeat the process.

It's important that if she does get up that you return her to where you placed her in the stay. She needs to understand that you expect her to stay in the location.

Once you have mastered the step backwards, we are going to repeat the process.

Always begin by putting her in a sit, then stay, and then move backward. Each time hold your step backward and frontward just a few seconds longer, then click, treat and release with an OK.

Always release with the same word and always release. The stay command doesn't end until you issue the release word.

This is an important aspect of your training because there may be times when you place your dog in a stay and have left her immediate area. A well trained dog will never leave her stay position until she is released with that word.

When you begin to see progress and your pauses between steps have lasted 3-5 seconds, it is time to increase your distance.

Now, instead of one step, take 2-3 steps backwards, pause briefly and return, click, treat and release.

As we increase distance, we will decrease the initial pause before you return. You do not want to entice her to move toward. The goal is to show her you will return to her if she just stays in place.

Practicing the release

The release is just as important as the stay command itself. Once you are able to have her stay while taking 2-3 steps backwards, we want to change the process slightly. This time, put her in a stay position, take your 2-3 steps backwards, step forwards and now instead of releasing, give a gentle praise, "Good Girl!", and repeat the process taking your 2-3 steps backwards and forwards. Now click, treat and release.

This little dance will teach her that just because you return doesn't mean she should come out of her stay position. There may be times when you put her in a stay and will need to pass by or near your dog. In doing so, you don't want her to move until you give her the release command.

Another very important thing to remember is to never release her from a stay from a distance. You should always release when you're close and always with the same word.

This is helpful because there also may be times when you put your dog in a stay in a public place. People may approach your dog, pet her, speak to her, etc., and you will want to make sure she will always remain in her stay position until only you release her.

Continue to practice the stay command and slowly increase your distance. Day 8 brings learning the stay with lots of distance.

Chapter 12

Day 8 – Stay Here, I'm Going Far Away

Day 8 has arrived and by now you should already see a huge difference in your dog. She's now sitting, lying down, coming when called and even beginning to stay in one place when you ask her.

Now the biggest of all tasks - having her stay while you move out of sight.

The "Stay" command by itself is very powerful. It builds trust between you and your dog, and you must rely on that trust to make it through the next stage.

Today you are going to put your dog in a "Stay" and then move a long distance and out of sight.

What you need: Clicker, treats, leash and patience.

Again, you're going to need a bit of patience with this one and you may just need to repeat day 7 until your dog has caught on that you will be returning to her so she doesn't have to move.

To begin, we are going to put her in a "Stay", take our 3-5 steps away, come back, click, treat and release. Think of this as a warm-up or reminder for her from yesterday.

Next we will put her in a stay again, but instead of stepping backward, we want to turn our back and walk away approximately 5 steps. Turn back toward her, pause, and walk back. Now click, treat and release.

Repeat this several times. Remember if she moves, simply move her back to where you left her, tell her to stay, and move away again.

We are now building up our ability to move away with her understanding that we will return. Each time you repeat the process, move a step further away, but always remain in sight. You may even wish to practice returning to her, giving a small treat (without clicking) or giving her a "Good Girl" and moving away again. If you do this remember, you didn't release her so she should still stay as you move away again.

When you feel comfortable that she is staying from a distance, it's now time to move out of sight. I find that this training is done best in the house as you can move into another room or even down the hall and quickly move her back to position if needed.

To begin moving out of sight, put her in a stay, turn your back and walk away. JUST BEFORE you leave her sight, turn toward her, gently tell her to stay again, and continue moving a way.

Stay out of sight for only a few seconds, come back into sight, reiterate the stay command and move out of sight again. Only stay there for a second or so, and then return to her, click, treat and release.

If you've made it this far and she hasn't moved you are doing great!

Even if she has moved it's OK. Dogs are curious and it will be natural for her to want to follow you. Simply reset and continue with your training.

Always be patient and always reset. Remember to never end the command without releasing her.

Adding Distractions

Since you've now been able to get her to stay put even when you've moved to another room, it may be time to add a few distractions.

This next task is always good to see just how disciplined she really is.

Grab a tennis ball or some other toy and have it ready.

Put her in a stay, move about 5-10 steps away and play with the toy, bounce the ball or cause some other distraction. It could even be someone knocking at the door.

As you bounce the ball or squeak the toy, gently and quietly reiterate the stay command. If she stays, give her a gentle "Good girl" or other praise, but do not click or treat at this time.

If she moves toward the distraction, reset and practice your stay command some more.

A well trained dog will ignore all distractions, even if it's her favorite toy.

If she makes it past a few ball bounces or squeaks, go back to her, click, treat, release and give her the toy. Remember, never release from a distance.

Congratulations! You've both just mastered the "Stay" command.

Chapter 13

Day 9 – Wait for Me

Have you noticed the moment you try and walk out the door with your dog she always jumps in front of you? Having your dog rush out the door can cause lots of problems and injuries. Trust me, I've seen it first-hand.

Imagine taking your 75lb Labrador Retriever for a walk and the moment the door is cracked open, she bolts out of the door, pulling you into the half opened door. OUCH!

I've known people this has happened to.

Not only will teaching this next command, "Wait", help with rushing out the door, it will teach your dog that you come first.

What you need: Clicker, treats, leash and an interior doorway.

I would strongly suggest starting this command using an interior doorway. It doesn't need to have an actual door on it, but that will help.

To begin, secure the leash to your dog. This is a great time to enforce the "Sit" command prior to putting the leash on her.

Keep only a short amount of leash available, so if you are using a 6 foot leash, be sure to choke up on the leash so there is only enough leash to keep her by your side and not stray ahead or behind you.

Release her from the sit and begin to walk through the doorway. She will naturally try and walk in front of you. If she does, pull her back and stop moving prior to moving through the doorway and say "Wait".

She may continue to surge through the door, however you must keep her back and stay in one place. We are teaching her patience. When she finally stops moving, say "Wait" and step forward through the doorway ahead of her. Once through the door, click, and give your release work while giving her a slight tug to follow you. Now treat.

It may take a few times for her to get the idea of what you are doing.

The reason we are treating at the very end is because giving her the immediate reward will break up the process and we also want her to follow us through the door after the release command.

As you continue this training it will look something like this:

Approach the doorway, give the "Wait" command while using the leash to pull her a step behind you, step in front of her, walk through the door, click, release and treat.

As you continue to practice this the moment you or anyone else approaches a door, you should be able to issue the "Wait" command, and she should stop in her tracks waiting for you and everyone else to continue ahead of her.

Going forward with all training and everyday activities, you should always issue a wait command before moving through a door or when you require her to pause and wait to be released.

The Wait command is different than the Stay command because you are not leaving her alone, you are simply expecting her to pause and wait for further instruction.

Now you are more than halfway to having that well-behaved dog you've dreamed of.

Remember to always reinforce your training sessions with everyday life routines.

Here are a few examples:

Always make your dog sit prior to attaching the leash.

At dinner time and rest time, always put your dog in a down or lie down position.

Before feeding, give a "Sit" or "Wait" command to prevent her from jumping at her food the moment it is placed on the floor.

Give the "Stay" command while moving to the next room to pick up an item or leaving her briefly.

Chapter 14

Day 10 – Don't Put That in Your Mouth

The Leave It Command

Many of these basic commands can really be used as life savers for your dog and the "Leave It" command is very powerful.

Puppies and curious dogs alike all jump at the opportunity to put things in their mouth that land on the floor. Nothing can be scarier than dropping some medicine, a sharp object like a thumbtack or anything else on the floor that could really harm your dog.

What you need: Clicker and treats

The "Leave It" command is used to deter your dog from picking something up off the floor, the table or anyplace else within reach.

Keep in mind that sometimes dogs will "counter surf" and jump up on the counters. The "Leave It" command shouldn't be used to get them off of the counter, that's the "Off" command.

To begin, we will want to clear away all of the other distractions from the floor in your training area.

Here is how the training exercise works.

You will be putting your dog in a sit command and then placing a small treat on the floor just outside of her reach. You will want her to be able to see it, but not reach it quickly.

I recommend using a treat that can be "squished" but that won't leave a mess on your floor or get broken if stepped on.

As soon as you place the treat on the floor you will want to tell her to "Leave it". At this time you should be standing right next to the treat and have your foot ready to "cover" the treat if she comes after it.

The best way to do this is keep your heel on the floor and toes/foot raised as if to show her what's under your foot, while covering the treat. (Actually your toes/foot will be slightly hovering over the treat.)

As she approaches the treat tell her again to "Leave It" and quickly cover the treat with your foot before she gets it.

Keep the treat covered with your foot until she backs away, then uncover the treat again.

Tell her to "Leave It" again. You may very well have to do this several times. Once she leaves the treat alone long enough for you to remove your foot, click, treat and pick up the treat on the floor.

We do not want her to take the treat we have been covering because that will teach her it is eventually ok to take what we are preventing her from having.

Now repeat the training.

Each time you put the treat on the floor you should be able to tell her to leave it. Eventually she will simply stare at the treat, inching closer, but she will not take it.

Once you can successfully tell her to leave the treat without her taking it, you can move on to dropping the treat on the floor and issuing the "Leave It" command to simulate a pill drop or something else more dangerous.

As she begins to understand the "Leave It" command, you can begin to drop her toys or other items on the floor giving the command. When she leaves them, ignores them or walks away, be sure to click and treat.

She's learning!

Chapter 15

Day 11 – Now That It's in There, Drop It!

The Drop It Command

The "Drop It" command is another very powerful and very handy command. As a puppy, she's likely going to put many, many things in her mouth, and it can be a constant battle to remove without getting bitten or drooled on.

Teaching this command will definitely help while training your dog, and if you happen to have lots of little things lying around your house, you will be able to keep things intact.

What you need: Clicker, treats and her favorite toy.

The difference between "Leave It" and "Drop It" is the possession. The "Leave It" command is used in anticipation of her grabbing something from the floor or table. "Drop It" will get that object freed from her mouth with ease.

To begin, we will need her favorite toy, a few small treats and the clicker. Make sure the toy is large enough for you to be able to grab it from her mouth, and that you will not have to pry her mouth open to get it.

Simply drop her toy and allow her to pick it up. She's going to naturally resist releasing it and giving it back to you. Take the hand with the treats and wave them in front of her nose. As you do this, say "Drop it".

She's going to now turn her interest toward the treats. The moment she drops the toy for the treat, click and reward. Be sure to then pick up the toy and continue the training.

Reinforcing this command is very simple. Just repeat the process.

This is also something that should be incorporated into a game of fetch or a game of tug.

Congratulations! You're on your way to having a well-behaved dog. Tomorrow you will be teaching her to go to her crate, bed or mat. This is where the magic happens.

Chapter 16

Day 12 – I Need Some Space

Sending Your Dog to Their Crate, Mat or Bed

This is a simple trick that can be used in many different scenarios and is a great help when you have guests come over or just to give yourself and your dog some space. You will also be able to use this command to help settle your dog for the night, prevent jumping on guests and give yourself some space during dinner time.

What you need: Clicker, treats, a bed, mat or crate.

The first step is to get your dog into her bed or on her mat in the down position. Having her lie down will come naturally to her and will help give her the idea that this is the place where she should rest and be calm.

To get her in on her mat or in her bed or crate, it's easiest to get her attention with a treat and place that treat on her bed. Once she's there, you can give her the "Down" command, click and treat.

This shows her where you want her to go.

Next, release her from her bed with the release word and move her away from the bed. Usually, just a few feet will be perfectly fine. We want her to recognize the action of moving toward her bed and getting on it.

Now this time we are going to give the command, "In your bed", while luring her to her bed with a treat, placing her in a down position, clicking and treating. Encourage her to stay in the bed a bit longer by giving another treat, but do not click.

You can release her at any time using your release word or phrase.

Continue to repeat the process by moving her out of her bed, then luring her back to the bed using a treat, giving the "In your bed" command and getting her to lie down. It's important that you are not clicking and treating for the down command itself, but rather the entire action.

Once she is reliably lying down you can move further away from her bed. Instead of luring her to the bed with a treat, simply issue the command. You should begin to see her moving toward the bed and lying down.

As soon as she is in the bed or on the mat, you will want her to lie down. If she does not, give her the "Down" command, then click and treat.

Add a hand signal by pointing to her bed or mat while giving the command.

Never send her to her bed, mat or crate and then discipline her. She will then begin to associate her bed with getting disciplined.

Repetition and consistency are the most important factors during these training sessions. Always be sure that each person helping to train your dog is giving the same commands, using the same hand signals, and always rewarding at the appropriate time.

Use the "In your bed" command every night and at least a few times a day just for reinforcement.

Tomorrow we will begin learning to talk a walk without being pulled around the streets.

Chapter 17

Day 13 – It's Time for a Walk

Leash walking can sometimes be a bit of a challenge, especially with larger dogs. In this chapter you are going to learn how to reward her for walking on a loose leash, without pulling, dragging or jumping.

What you need: Clicker, treats and a 6 foot leash. (Do not use a retractable leash)

It's important that during the leash walking training session that you do not use one of the retractable type leashes. These leashes keep a constant tension on the dogs' collar and we want her to get used to the feeling of a loose hanging leash.

Puppies and dogs that are not used to walking on a leash will often pull on the leash and take you for a walk. Some people will recommend choke collars, harnesses and even pronged collars. None of these contraptions are actually necessary if you train her to walk next to you with a loose leash.

During our leash training sessions, we are going to take slow, deliberate walks that will require your patience. You may find that it takes a very long time to go a short distance, but she will quickly learn what it is you are after and you will be well on your way to a completely pleasant and great paced walk.

To begin, you will want to keep your clicker and treats handy. I recommend a treat pouch so you will have quick access to treats during your walk.

Your goal during the walk is to have her by your side, not pulling you and not crossing in front of or behind you at any time.

Keeping her at your side, place her in a sit position with the leash on and allow the leash to hang loose while you are holding it firmly. You will only want enough of the leash available to fall by her side, but not enough for her to move more than 2 feet away from you.

Once she's in a sit, give her the release command, step forward, click, treat and give her praise with a "Good Girl or Boy!" If you are holding her on your left side you should click and treat with your right hand. At this time she will now give you attention because she is aware you have treats.

As you continue walking every few steps, give her praise, click and give her a treat. What you should find is that she will take a few steps and look up to you for a treat. If you can continue to walk, click and treat at the same time without breaking stride or pace it will be helpful. Otherwise, a short pause won't hurt.

If she begins to pull or stray, stop your walk immediately and wait. As soon as she give you attention again, sits or allows the leash to become slack, give her praise and begin walking again.

Occasionally you should give praise with a "Good Girl or Boy!", but do not give a treat. She should learn that praise is enough. Be sure not to click if you are only giving praise.

While you are continuing your walk, occasionally and randomly click and treat while giving her praise. You will also begin to see her occasionally looking up at you expecting praise. When she does, you know she's caught on.

That's all there is to mastering the loose leash walk! Congratulations!

Chapter 18

Day 14 – Putting it All Together

You've made it! It's your last day of training and by now you should have a well-behaved and trained dog. Just remember that each dog learns at their own pace. It is also important that you have dedicated the time with your dog over the last thirteen days to help them become that perfect well-behaved dog.

Of course, you will want to continue integrating each of your commands into your daily routine. Over time, you will see just how easy it is to control your perfect pet and how the two of you can easily coexist without problems.

Now it's time to put it all together.

Each day you should have integrated your training sessions into everyday life. Here are some ways you can use them each and every day to reinforce your dog's good behavior.

Feeding time
Prior to feeding your dog, put her in a sit and make her wait until you've place the food down. If she begins to move as you get closer to placing the food on the floor, simply pick up the food, give the sit and wait commands, and repeat. Each time she moves toward the food before you've fully placed it on the floor, pick it up and start over. Do not give her the food until she has waited for you to place the food on the floor and released her.
This is a great way to reinforce the "Wait" command.

Putting on the leash

Many dogs will go absolutely crazy the moment they see the leash. At that time it becomes a major chore to get the leash attached and get out of the door. Dogs learn by repetitive behavior and when you set some expectations for them you'll be amazed at what they can accomplish. Remember, you must be patient when training.

When putting on her leash you should put her in either a down or sit position. Once she is set, attach her leash. If she continues to jump, simply wait. Continue to put her in a down or sit position and attempt to attach her leash. Each time she moves, cease putting her leash on and reset. You'll be surprised how quickly she will learn what's expected of her.

Wait at the door

Before you and your dog go through any door always give her the wait command and you should walk through first. This includes going for a walk or simply walking around the house. Also be sure to make her wait when entering the house as well.

The guests are here

When you have guests come to your house you should have your dog get used to going to her mat, bed or crate to "settle" before greeting any new guests. This will help with jumping and overly excited dogs. Practice this by having someone ring the doorbell. As soon as the doorbell rings send her to her bed, mat or crate. Continue to train her in this way and soon guests will love to visit instead of shying away from your dog.

Don't forget your bonus chapter that contains more tips and tricks. Download it for free today at *http://wellbehavedin14days.com*

Chapter 19

Next Steps for Training

Now that you have your well-behaved dog you need to make sure that you always give praise and encourage her even when you are not in "training" mode. Give her a "Good Girl!", when she sits quietly next to you or when she looks back at you when walking on a leash.

A little praise goes a long way and shows her that you would rather have her behaving and receiving good attention than scolding her for bad attention.

Since your dog now understands how the clicker works, and you have continuously reinforced the "Look at me!" command throughout training, new tricks will be a breeze.

If you're ready to move on to a few more challenging tricks be sure to download your free bonus chapter from http://wellbehavedin14days.com.

In the bonus chapter you'll discover some additional fun tricks to teach your dog and show off to your family and friends.

Did you enjoy the training? Be sure to provide a review and tell others how much you enjoyed the training. Leave your review here: http://wellbehavedin14days.com/reviews

31490770R00036

Made in the USA
Lexington, KY
14 April 2014